CHINESE NEW YEAR

By
Shalini Vallepur

BookLife
PUBLISHING

©2019
BookLife Publishing Ltd.
King's Lynn
Norfolk, PE30 4LS

All rights reserved.
Printed in Malaysia.

A catalogue record for this
book is available from the
British Library.

ISBN: 978-1-78637-807-1

Written by:
Shalini Vallepur

Edited by:
Madeline Tyler

Designed by:
Drue Rintoul

Photo Credits

All images are courtesy of Shutterstock.com. With thanks to Getty Images, Thinkstock Photo and iStockphoto. Front Cover – Olga_C. 2–3 – TOMO. 4–5 – 1981 Rustic Studio kan, wong sze yuen. 6–7 – szefei, Toa55. 8–9 – Kochkanyan Juliya, Lukasz Szwaj. 10–11 – PR Image Factory, LDWYTN. 12–13 – wong yu liang, Xianghong Garrison, Tom Wang. 14–15 – Krunja, szefei. 16–17 – Eastfenceimage, bonchan. 18–19 – CHEN WS, crazybike. 20–21 – Dan Hanscom, En min Shen. 22–23 – Kobby Dagan, 1981 Rustic Studio kan.

CONTENTS

Words that look like <u>this</u> can be found in the glossary on page 24.

CELEBRATE CHINESE NEW YEAR WITH ME!

Xin Nian Kuai Le! This means 'Happy New Year' in Mandarin. My name is Li An. I'm here to tell you about Chinese New Year.

It sounds like this: 'shin nee-an kwai le'.

Chinese New Year is sometimes called the Spring Festival. We say goodbye to winter and welcome spring. It is a time for families to come together and wish for good <u>fortune</u>.

CHINESE NEW YEAR

We celebrate Chinese New Year in late January or in February. The date can change because we wait for a new moon. This is when you can't see the Moon in the sky on a clear night.

Chinese New Year is also a time
to remember our <u>ancestors</u>.
It has been celebrated in
China for around 4,000 years.

THE STORY OF CHINESE NEW YEAR

A long time ago, there was a monster called Nian. Nian lived in the mountains high above a village.

Nian would wake up on New Year's Day every year and attack the village. The terrible monster would eat all the food and animals, and even scare the children!

Every New Year's Eve, the villagers hid from Nian in their houses.

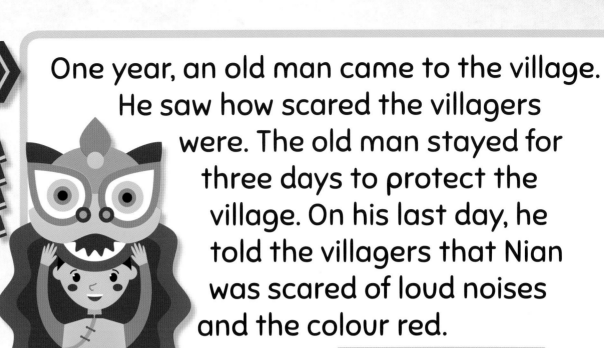

One year, an old man came to the village. He saw how scared the villagers were. The old man stayed for three days to protect the village. On his last day, he told the villagers that Nian was scared of loud noises and the colour red.

On New Year's Eve, the villagers lit fireworks and <u>firecrackers</u>. They hung red <u>lanterns</u> in the streets and all the children wore masks.

大吉大利

新年快乐

心

It worked! Nian did not come down from the mountains that night or ever again.

9

GET READY TO CELEBRATE

We start getting ready about a week before New Year's Day. We get ready for the new year by cleaning our homes. It's important that we get rid of any dust and bad luck.

We decorate our houses with lots of red things. Red is a lucky colour that brings us happiness and good fortune. We hang decorations such as red knots and red lanterns.

NEW YEAR'S EVE

New Year's Eve is a day for family. People who live away from their parents travel back for New Year's Eve. I love New Year's Eve because everybody comes together and we have a huge feast.

We also put up poems called spring couplets. We write the poems on red paper and hang them up in doorways. Lots of buildings have spring couplets outside for everybody to see.

Couplets

13

NEW YEAR'S DAY

After we eat our feast, we stay up to wait for <u>midnight</u>. At midnight, fireworks go off and we light firecrackers. Everything is colourful and loud to scare Nian away, just like in the story.

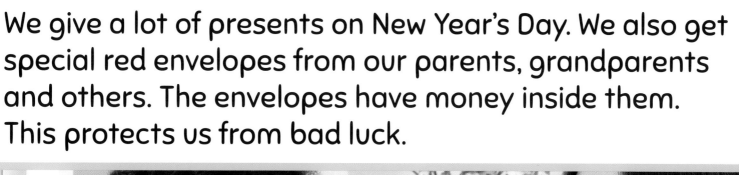

We give a lot of presents on New Year's Day. We also get special red envelopes from our parents, grandparents and others. The envelopes have money inside them. This protects us from bad luck.

Some people send money to their friends on phone apps.

15

FESTIVE FOOD

In some parts of China, it is a <u>tradition</u> for families to make and eat dumplings together. The Chinese word for dumpling is 'jiaozi' and it means 'changing of the year'. Perfect for Chinese New Year!

Sweet rice balls are a tradition in some parts of China. They are made from a special rice powder and filled with sugar, fruits or nuts.

Rice balls are said to bring families together.

THE LANTERN FESTIVAL

After New Year's Day, families may spend the next week visiting <u>relatives</u> and friends. The Lantern Festival begins when the next full moon arrives and marks the end of Chinese New Year celebrations.

The streets are lined with lots of lanterns!

We all go outside to see the lanterns.
We also watch the dragon and lion dances.
Long dragons are carried on sticks and <u>swirled</u>
around by skilled dancers. It is an amazing show!

Some dragons can be 60 metres long.

THE CHINESE ZODIAC

When the new year starts, there will be a new zodiac sign. The zodiac signs are 12 animals. Each animal means a different thing – people born in the year of the rat are said to be kind and smart.

Can you spot the year you were born?
What is your Chinese zodiac animal?

RAT
2008, 2020

OX
2009, 2021

TIGER
2010, 2022

RABBIT
2011, 2023

DRAGON
2012, 2024

SNAKE
2013, 2025

HORSE
2014, 2026

GOAT
2015, 2027

MONKEY
2016, 2028

ROOSTER
2017, 2029

DOG
2018, 2030

PIG
2019, 2031

If you were born at the end of January or in February, you may need to double-check what your Chinese zodiac sign is.

CHINESE NEW YEAR AROUND THE WORLD

Chinese New Year celebrations take place all around the world because many Chinese people live outside China. There is a big celebration in California in the US every year where millions of people watch a <u>parade</u>.

I hope you have enjoyed learning all about Chinese New Year. Why not see if there are any Chinese New Year celebrations that happen where you live?

GLOSSARY

ancestors	people in a family who lived a long time ago
firecrackers	small tubes that make loud noises when lit
fortune	a person's luck
lanterns	lights covered in paper that come in different shapes
midnight	twelve o'clock at night
parade	when people walk or dance down a street with others watching
relatives	members of the same family
swirled	moved in a twisting pattern
tradition	a belief or action that is passed down between people over time

INDEX

24